# *What's Your Story?*

# *What's Your Story?*

## Discover the Man Behind Your Dad

Mike Lindstrom

Vincent Staniforth

A POST HILL PRESS BOOK

ISBN: 978-1-68261-072-5

ISBN (eBook): 978-1-68261-073-2

WHAT'S YOUR STORY?

Discover the Man Behind Your Dad

© 2016 by Vincent Staniforth and Mike Lindstrom

All Rights Reserved

Cover Design by Quincy Alivio

Post Hill Press

275 Madison Avenue, 14th Floor

New York, NY 10016

posthillpress.com

# Contents

# Acknowledgements

WE WOULD LIKE TO thank our parents for giving us the gift of life and the opportunity for us to encourage other parents to share their life stories with their children. We would like to thank our families above all; our wives Monica and Vivienne, our sons, Rhett, Colt, Conor, and Harley that have encouraged us along the entire journey. Special thank you from Mike to "Grams" Madelon Griblin for totally being there for me and the Boys, especially when I needed to steal away hours to write—love you more than I express. Skip Lindstrom, Doug Glass and Mike Greco for their contributions. To Treg Balding, Jeffrey Marx and Coach Ehrmann for sharing your story in 2008 and ultimately being the people that brought us together from across The Pond to write this book. To Dan Lier, Tony Robbins and Josh Jenkins-Robbins for helping me (Mike) start down this path of personal development back in La Jolla, CA in 1998; what's written is definitely for REAL! To all of our clients that have been understanding with our time and schedules when our passion for this message was so pressing. We want to thank our publishing team at Post Hill Press for believing in us when others doubted.

# *Foreword*

## Vincent Staniforth:

In October 1990, my father passed away suddenly. Aside from the hammer-blow shock of the event and the long process of grieving for a man I deeply loved, I felt constantly frustrated by the knowledge that I would never have the chance to learn more about his life, his dreams and his hard-earned wisdom. That frustration drove me, some years later, to write a book called *Questions for My Father*. I wanted to see if I could craft something that would offer a way for children and Dads to start a conversation, to make a vehicle to carry a Dad's stories and make them available for all time. It was my first experience of writing a book, seeing it published and watching it exist in the real world rather than having it rattle around in my head, and I have to say it was an odd time. I wasn't prepared for the strangeness of promoting a book that proclaimed, in very clear, unambiguous language, to the whole wide world: "I blew it. Here's an idea to help avoid the same mistake." It didn't help when I saw a *New Yorker* cartoon showing a man looking at his laptop, speaking into a phone and saying, "I can't do Tuesday. I'm in Chicago merchandising my pain." It made me laugh and cringe at the same time—was that me? Was I just another wannabe author, schilling my angst in a world of media sound bites and microsecond attention spans? And then there was the time I was doing a book signing in a suburban mall in Texas. Two teenage boys passed my table and the banner sporting the book's title. Without breaking stride, one of the boys turned to his buddy and said loudly, "Right. *Dad, why are you such an asshole?*"

At the other end of the spectrum, a reader in New Zealand wrote to tell me that her father had taken the book and *within its pages* had written his answers to all of its questions. A family treasure had been created and she had written to thank me for taking my experience and putting it to good use.

And so the book made its way in the world, and life carried on. For a long time I only thought about the book when I'd see it on a shelf when searching for another title. Reading it now, with the clarity of hindsight and time long passed, it's clear I was in a great deal of pain when I wrote those words, and I feel bad for that younger version of myself, struggling with a young family in a new country, carrying all the worries and uncertainties familiar to any parent. I want to give him a hug and tell him things will work out, mostly for the better.

But life is a journey, and we gather both scars and successes along the way. In late 2014, with both our boys grown and pursuing their own adventures, my wife and I returned to England. During that uncertain and stressful process of packing up our life in America and transposing it to England, I thought about my Dad and the book a great deal. I found myself wondering aloud if it had any relevance any more—if it ever had any, indeed—and thought about how much my perspective had changed now that I am an older Dad. I felt that somehow I had missed something in the book that was elemental to the whole experience of being a Dad and being a son and working through that whole complex, critical relationship. There was something about the passing of stories from one generation to another that kept tugging at my sleeve; in my book I had focused totally on the *questions* we need to ask, but I wasn't sure I had properly explored the idea of *the stories* those questions should evoke.

Then one evening I received a LinkedIn message from some guy called Mike Lindstrom, asking if perhaps there was a way to further develop my original idea into something more in tune with current times and challenges. *Well, well*, I thought—*scars and successes*. Our email correspondence turned into long phone calls and it quickly became apparent that Mike "got" what I was trying to do back in 1998, and had a tremendous passion for moving it forward. At the end of one of those long conversations, I remember saying to Mike, "For me it comes down to this: *Storytelling is an act of love*." Mike agreed, and the result is the book you are now reading. I hope it serves you well and helps you find the stories in your life that need to be told.

## Mike Lindstrom:

In 2008, my wife and I were expecting our first child and mid-pregnancy we learned we were having a boy. Growing up with no older brothers, my Dad and I spent so much time together doing "boy things." Playing baseball, building forts in the house, going camping, learning to "make a fist," going fishing, etc. so I always envisioned myself having a little boy as my own first child. Needless to say I was over the moon when the sonogram showed that little stub between his legs. Like any excited father-to-be, I started sharing the news with all of my friends and clients. With the exciting news comes a lot of advice from other fathers that have been down the road I was about to embark. I took it all in and always considered the source of the advice giver but there were a few very impactful ones that stood out to me.

One of those impactful father friends was a friend named Treg. He was a highly successful sales professional in the insurance industry and a father of three himself (two boys and a girl). He had all of the attributes of a "man's man": tall, square jaw, great looking athletic type, with a lot of swagger but it was always Treg's character that stood out to me. Words like authentic, compassionate and a confidant is how I saw him. So when I go to my mailbox one day and I see a book and a letter from Treg indicating this is a must read for me as a father to be, I didn't ask any questions. That book was *Season of Life* by Jeffrey Marx. Admittedly, at the time I didn't know much about the book but had heard of it from some athlete friends of mine. On the inside cover, there was a handwritten note from Treg that said:

*11/6/07*

*Michael,*

*Wanted to share this book that has touched me deeply. Your friendship is very special to me and I love you as a Brother. God Bless.*

> *Proverbs 20:7*
> *The just man walketh in his integrity; his children are blessed after him.*

*Treg*

Needless to say, I dove into the book that afternoon and read it in less than 3 hours. The bestselling inspirational book in which the author reunites with a childhood football hero, now a minister and coach, and witnesses a revelatory demonstration of the true meaning of manhood. Joe Ehrmann, a former NFL football star and volunteer coach for the Gilman high school football team, teaches his players the keys to successful defense: penetrate, pursue, punish, love. A former captain of the Baltimore Colts and now an ordained minister, Ehrmann is serious about the game of football but even more serious about the purpose of life. *Season of Life* is his inspirational story as told by Pulitzer Prize–winning journalist Jeffrey Marx, who was a ball boy for the Colts when he first met Ehrmann.

Ehrmann now devotes his life to teaching young men a whole new meaning of masculinity. He teaches the boys at Gilman the precepts of his "Building Men for Others" program: Being a man means emphasizing relationships and having a cause bigger than yourself. It means accepting responsibility and leading courageously. It means that empathy, integrity, and living a life of service to others are more important than points on a scoreboard. Decades after he first met Ehrmann, Jeffrey Marx renewed their friendship and watched his childhood hero putting his principles into action. While chronicling a season with the Gilman Greyhounds, Marx witnessed the most extraordinary sports program he'd ever seen, where players say "I love you" to each other and coaches profess their love for their players. Off the field Marx sat with Ehrmann and absorbed life lessons that led him to re-examine his own unresolved relationship with his father. *Season of Life* is a book about what it means to be a man of substance and impact. It is a moving story that will resonate with athletes, coaches, parents—anyone struggling to make the right choices in life.

The book moved me in so many ways but there was one big thing Marx mentions in the book on page 101 that literally changed my life. Marx mentions another book titled *Questions for My Father* by Vincent Staniforth. It's a book that shares a powerful exercise of interviewing one's own father while they are still alive in order to learn his life's entire story. I immediately drove straight to Barnes and Noble in Scottsdale and requested a copy of *Questions for My Father*. It was hugely disappointing that not only did they not have a copy but that the book had been out of print. My best chance was to go on Amazon and get a re-purposed copy or used copy of the book online. I went online and found the book and had it shipped immediately.

Dating back to 1998, when I worked as a professional coach and a performance consultant for famed author and speaker, Tony Robbins, I was a "journaler." I remember, as a performance coach for Tony's company, Robbins Results Partnership, his son and friend of mine, Josh Jenkins-Robbins, and I always had our journals within feet of us at all times. If anyone ever showed up to a meeting with Tony without a journal or notebook, it was almost like it sent a message that, "I am not serious about being here and learning."

Tony would beat us up with this one simple phrase that I still use to this day, "What is planned is only possible and what's written is REAL!" From that point on I found myself chronicling anything from a business meeting to a coaching session to my own personal thoughts on the world. I came up with this idea to track down this *Questions for My Father* and copy the questions in the book into a journal so I could fill it in and write my own life story to our first son to be, Rhett Michael Lindstrom due in the Summer of 2008. The book arrived on my doorstep and so began a 12-month journey to answer some 150 questions as given to me by the author Vincent Staniforth. Some questions were easy one-liners and many more questions forced me to dig into my own childhood and share my life experiences. It was so therapeutic for me that it prompted me to think of my own questions to answer and share with my future son.

As a frequent traveler for my speaking events, I am on airplanes quite a bit. On one flight as I was writing the answers into my journal, there was bad turbulence and I had a surreal *"what if?"* moment. *"What if this plane was to go down and my baby son wouldn't know all of these things trapped in my mind?"* Needless to say, this created a lot of urgency for me to finish the journal/questions so it could remain in a safe place (in a safety deposit box where it sits today).

While on stage at a sales summit as the keynote speaker during that first year of my son's life, an audience member asked me a question, "Can you share any strategies of ways to being a better parent?" I was a little taken aback by the question because this was a sales training session and, moreover, I am NO parenting expert by any stretch of the imagination. I paused while I gathered my thoughts, then shared my story of me writing a full journal to my baby boy based on the book *Questions for My Father.* I was amazed by the reaction sharing an off-the-cuff exercise triggered. People had tears in their eyes, they shared stories with me and at least a dozen professional men came up and hugged me, thanking me for sharing my story and that they too were going to buy Vincent's book and write to their own children. I realized something special was just born in my own life and career as a professional speaker and coach. I knew that I had to tell this story and help other people learn their own parents'/families' stories.

That year during my annual goal-setting retreat in December, I wrote down the goal in my plan "To contact Vincent Staniforth and rewrite *Questions for My Father* and co-author it together." As life will have it, there were some twists and turns in my own life. I wrote my first book in 2010, I had my second son (Colt) in 2011 and my business was growing as my time was diminishing. In January of 2015, as I wrote down my annual goals, that long-standing overdue goal was still starring me down this year after 5 years: "To contact Vincent Staniforth and rewrite *Questions for My Father* and co-author it together." I told myself in that moment that it would be this year 2015 or I was going to cross it off the plan and let it go. Keep in mind, Vincent and I had never met and I didn't even know if he cared to re-write what he had already put in print in 1998. In previous years, I was unsuccessful at tracking Vincent down so I always viewed that as a sign that it wasn't meant to be. "This was going to be the year," I said again.

Up late on a Saturday night at my house, I went on LinkedIn and saw his profile and also an email address for him. I couldn't believe it! I starred at his profile for a long time and pondered whether or not to write that long overdue letter to Vincent. Well, I let my courage voice win out and I sent it on Sunday, January 25, 2015 at 12:14 am MT:

*Vincent,*

*I found your info on LinkedIn this past week. I am a professional speaker and author in Scottsdale, AZ and I am working on some new writing projects here in 2015 and have been wanting to connect with you for some time. I read your book when my wife was pregnant with our son Rhett (now 6 1/2 years old) and it impacted me immensely. So much so that I talk about your book in the majority of my live events when I am talking to professional parents. I challenge Dads in my audiences to write a full journal to their children and now with video technology, my message to parents has become even more powerful in their communication with their children. I can explain more when we talk.*

*I wanted to see if you and I could jump on a phone call as I have an idea that I think you might like to help update and revitalize the message of your book in a whole new way in 2015. I am friends with a lot of the big name authors/speakers*

*here in the US and I am confident we, together,*
*could create something powerful for people that*
*picks up on where you started with Questions for*
*My Father. I see you are a busy professional from*
*your LinkedIn profile—I have been passionate*
*about this idea for a while but, candidly, didn't*
*have the proper time I wanted to commit to it and*
*now I do.*

*Feel free to search some of my info below. I*
*started in the speaking world working directly for*
*Tony Robbins fresh out of law school back in 1998*
*and have broadened my brand ever since. I really*
*hope we can connect and discuss this together.*

*Thanks so much!*
*Mike*

After I hit the send button, I felt relieved
but I felt more anxiety asking all of these bad
questions. What if he doesn't respond? What if
he doesn't want to write this with me? What if
I offend him implying his original work wasn't

good enough and needed to be improved? I could see on his profile that he was in the UK these days so midnight my time, he should see this email on a Sunday morning. I went to bed with my thoughts racing. I woke up on Sunday morning with no response so now my self-talk was really getting negative. I remember that Sunday morning sitting in church and my wife kept nudging me to quit checking my cell phone and listen to the Pastor. I was indeed checking my email like every 5 minutes for the entire hour. I even prayed in church that day to "show me a sign one way or another" on this goal I had set 6 years previous. I figured being in church on Sunday and being a God-fearing man that surely the man upstairs would communicate me with somehow. Church ended, no email and I am walking back to my car with my two sons in tow and my cell phone vibrates indicating a new message. I started shaking and getting nervous like a high school student about to open a letter from their desired college accepting or rejecting them. I looked down and it was from Vincent Staniforth. I kept reading still nervous and it said:

*Mike—I'm on the road right now but would love to connect.*

*Best,*
*Vin*

I hadn't felt that unique kind of excitement in some time and I knew in that moment this book was meant to be. God did "wink" at me that Sunday morning. A week later, "Vin," as I now know my good friend and co-author, and I met and spoke for the first time on a telephone call. We were both so excited to connect, we shared ideas back and forth, shared about our personal lives and the rest is history, as the saying goes.

# *How to Use this Book*

So much has changed since the original book *Questions for My Father* came out in 1998; namely the furiously fast growth of the Internet, the birth of social media and its associated me-too technology. When the original version of the book was conceived, it was meant to help create a conversation between a father and his children. As you read in the foreword, when Mike first read *Questions for My Father*, he took it one step further by transcribing all of the questions from the book into an empty journal and writing the answers to his first newborn son. In our appearances and/or trainings over the years, we learned that a lot of parents (namely fathers for the sake of this book) loved the idea of writing out the answers to their children but found it difficult to take the time to manually write out that much content. As such we wanted to incorporate some easy-to-follow strategies to help father's make this powerful process easier all around.

The direction you might take with these questions will be guided by your own age and whether or not your father is still alive and has the mental capacity to fully engage in the conversation. Here are some scenarios you might consider when approaching the questions:

WRITTEN JOURNAL

The first thing we want anyone to do before writing or interviewing is to take a deep breath and *think*. For most people, actively stepping back from any situation and appraising it objectively is pretty difficult; we are driven by technology, social media and the pressures of 21st century life to *react* rather than *think, then act*. Much of the tech that we use to engage in the modern world is designed to help us move faster and act quicker than ever before—and a lot of it is useful and has positive benefits, to be sure. But this is a special journey you're about to start; it deserves some undivided, considered attention.

Taking a few brief minutes to look at this book and think about how you are going to start your journey will make a big difference, because the very first part of telling a story is taking the time to think about *how* you're going to tell the story; what tone will you use? Are you going to highlight the drama in your stories or the humor? Are you going to tell those stories that carry a message, that illustrate how you have learned your own lessons in life? Or are you going to set your mind free and tell the stories that come naturally? Taking the time to reflect on these questions will, we promise, enhance your experience and help you share the stories that really make a difference to your loved ones.

The next step is to invest in a robust, quality journal and use the questions in the book as your prompt to elicit the answers from your own father. For those fathers that have children, the same can be done by writing into the journal the responses as a keepsake for your own kids. In the case of Mike, he is fortunate to have both his father still alive and he has two young sons. In this scenario, imagine how emotionally powerful it is to have your own father's answers and to also be proactive and write to your own children as a gift. Mike's sons will have two generations of family history to have and hold as they mature and grow into young men. As an illustration, when Mike asked his own father, Skip, if he had to boil it down to his top questions to be addressed, this is what he came up with below. These questions started the dialogue between the two of them and they are now reduced to a journal locked up in a safety deposit box as a family keepsake.

1. How was growing up in the 50s and 60s different than it is for kids today?

2. What are you afraid of?

3. As you look back, who had the biggest impact on your early life (negative and positive)?

4. What is the BEST & WORST decision that you ever made?

5. Who was your greatest mentor(s)/coach(s) growing up (as a kid or teenager)?

6. Who taught you the most growing up? What did you learn from that person?

7. What single event had the greatest impact on you as a child?

8. What are the "highlight" grandparent stories that you remember?

9. What grandparents do you admire most and why?

10. What did you fail to accomplish in life that you always wanted?

11. What's one thing that you want to do before you die?


AUDIO RECORDING

Many readers from the original book used the questions to facilitate a face-to-face sit down where they interviewed their father and audio recorded the entire questions series. Whether it was in one sitting or a series of meetings, they were able to not only capture the essence of the responses but were able to preserve the father in his own voice. The people that preferred this method found it took less time than the journaling method. We have a reader that shared how he used this method to schedule actual "Dates with Dad" and it brought them extremely close over the time he recorded these conversations. There are some great inexpensive audio recording devices that can record digitally rather than have tapes or DVDs that might be lost or destroyed over time.

MIKE: I remember having some basic historical questions to ask my "Pop" (my mom's father, Ray Lenczewski) back in 2000-01 when he was in his 80's. He lived in a small apartment alone in Sacramento, CA. My grandmother had passed away some years before and my Pop was coping with life without the woman he loved his whole life. I wanted to take the time to just have a conversation with him about his life, missing my grandmother ("Nana" as we called her), growing up during The Depression, being Polish and being a steel worker in Chicago, IL, his beliefs about politics and religion, etc. He was very willing to share his "story" with me one-on-one (mind you, this was before I had this book in mind nor had read Vincent's original book from 1998 *Questions for My Father.*) There was one simple caveat my Pop told me, "You can ask me anything you want but I don't want that damn video camera on me when I share." At that time, I was invested in the video, virtual tour, camera world at that time in my consulting career with a company called bamboo.com/ipix.com. This was the "dot-com era" that I was a part of in Northern California so I figured my Pop would enjoy the new technology (at that time). Not so much! He demanded I shut off the video and place an old school audio tape recording device in front of us to have the conversation. Of course, I respected his wishes and recorded an hour of simple historical questions on a Sony micro-cassette device.

We share this for a reason! You may be a 28-year-old millennial looking to follow our system of questions. Your smart phone might be looked at unkindly from your 60-year-old father or 85-year old grandfather. We believe the journal strategy is the least invasive and most comfortable—and it's important to ask your father (or grandfather) what they are most comfortable with in terms of the conversation.

VIDEO RECORDING

Let's face it; video is king. Anyone, regardless of age or skill, can shoot a video on a smart phone and upload them to various places on the Internet: YouTube, Facebook, Instagram, Pinterest, Google+, etc. Some view us, as writers, a bit "old school" because we actually enjoy hunkering down in a small coffee shop for hours at a time and let the pen fill up a journal with the handwritten word. At the same time, as we wrote this book we very much understood addressing the video recording medium as an additionally effective method to preserving the answers to our questions.

We have seen this done a couple ways. First, similar to the audio recording method, set up a date or series of dates and record your conversations with your father. The other way we have seen dads use the video recording strategy is to record themselves answering the questions to their own children over several smaller takes. One dad in particular put a weekly reminder on his calendar every Sunday afternoon to take 15 minutes and answer the questions into his iPhone with the aim of gifting the final recordings to his two teenage kids when they turned 18 years of age. As we all know, technology is ever changing so whether you do an audio or video recording, it is important to have it uploaded somewhere for safe keeping as you record it (like a cloud, a free YouTube channel or a similar online storage in case the device was ever lost or stolen). We both have lost timeless pictures or small smart phone videos because they were not backed up in another location online.

Regardless of what strategy you decide to utilize, make the full commitment that you will go through all of the questions included in the list and set a specific date to complete them by. If you are a father yourself, it is great if you can have two opportunities to use this book, assuming you are fortunate to have both your father and your children alive to share. We have so many supporters and friends as we wrote the book that didn't have the ability to ask their own father these questions because they had passed along. As such, these fathers were even more motivated and excited to make sure their own kids had this blueprint of their lives for generations to come. We know that the emphasis of this book is for fathers and yet we have seen people take these questions and interview their grandparents or even other family members.

# The Power of Questions, the Power of Stories

## LESSON LEARNED

VINCENT: It was a full nine years after my dad died that I stopped confusing *thinking* about doing things differently with *actually* doing them; it was time to talk to Mum about her life and make sure her stories weren't lost to memory. One evening I sat her down and started a conversation with my list of prepared questions. A lot of them were to do with her childhood in Ireland—I really wanted to get a sense of time and place, to build a picture of the girl and young woman called Margaret before she became *Mum* instead. It was fascinating listening to her, to see her completely engaged in the moment as she recalled child-hood events. Within a couple of minutes Mum lost her initial reticence about talking with a tape recorder between us on the table.

The conversation quickly strayed beyond the narrow channels suggested by my questions. I felt a real sense of being taken along for a trip back in time. *Listen to me. Hear my stories. I need to tell you what it was like leaving the farm in Ireland as a teenager, the childhood death of a younger brother, of working in munitions factories during the war, of becoming a nurse, of living a life in my own right before I met your Dad.*

It was an enthralling experience. And it was all there on tape, and later, in a transcription. I was able to share with my brother and sisters and their children. But here's the question I've been dodging: Why did it take so long for me to put the recording project into action in the first place? Hadn't I learned anything from leaving it too late with my Dad? Here's my answer: I believe there is an unspoken admission, by both parties concerned, that these stories being told are for posterity, as a way of being able to relate to a loved one after their passing—and that's a tough barrier to overcome. I know I was uncomfortable with approaching my Mum with a tape recorder and a list of questions—but the experience of leaving it too late to hear my Dad's stories provided the necessary impetus.

It's many years now since my Mum passed away. Every so often I will read the transcript of my interview with her, or if I want to hear her soft, lilting accent again I will play the recording, close my eyes and be taken to another place. Listening to her stories. Listening to her *love*.

WHO'S TEACHING WHO?
("*And shouldn't that be 'whom', Dad?*")

VINCENT: Sometimes I think the total of my wisdom as a father of two sons, now in their twenties, can be written in big letters on the back of a postage stamp. There is no point at which, as a thinking Dad, you can sit back and say, *"There. Done it, job complete. Made a couple of wrong moves but in the end we all got through that child-raising thing in one piece."* Nope, not for one second. The whole machine is always in motion, always evolving, always surprising. There are quiet times to be sure, moments when you can catch a breath and collect yourself for the next day, the next adventure, the next challenge. So maybe that's one piece of wisdom I've learned—the knowledge that being a Dad, to borrow a phrase, isn't just for Christmas; it's for life.

But there's been another kind of wisdom learned along the journey. My Dad died before either of my two sons was born, so their only knowledge of him came from me and the stories they've heard from their aunts and uncles. Just think about that for a second; those two boys now have a clear, engaging picture of a grandfather they've never met *because of the stories people told.*

Over the years I've tried to make good, in my own way, on a promise I made that my sons would be able to talk to me about anything, and I could tell them anything in return if it went towards building a positive, two-way communication channel. There were times when it was uncomfortable to hear what they had to say; but the journey goes on and we have had, and continue to have, some of the most rewarding and beautiful conversations I can imagine. I've told my stories, I've listened to their stories, and together we know and understand each other in a way that, to me, is priceless. Looking back I can see that, where fatherhood is concerned, I've had three great teachers; my Dad and my two boys.

## LETTER FROM A READER

*Dear Mr. Staniforth,*

*Last month my dad sent me your book,* Questions
for my Father, *as a Christmas present. When
I opened it at first I thought it was a nice
inspirational book about Dads. I read my Dad's
words he had penned in the front for me, had a big
cry and put the book away to read later.*

*Eating breakfast this morning I thought I'd
have a look at the book. As I opened the book
and saw my Dad's writing I could not believe the
treasure I held in my hands! I wept as I read these
pages. My children, 5, 4 and 3 stared at me. My
oldest son said, "Mom, are you ok?" I said, "I
miss your Grandpa very much and I feel sad." He
hugged me and he cried a little too.*

*In my family I am the oldest, then I have a
younger sister (5 years younger). My Dad has
always been a loving, generous and compassionate*

man. He has always been good at communicating and has taught us girls to share our feelings and to love deeply.

In my Father's answers, I didn't read anything that shocked me or was a mystery. But what I do have is a written book of all the things I already knew. A book I can read whenever I want, a book to draw me close to him across the miles (he lives in Iowa, USA), a book my children can read some day to tell them about their grandfather.

My Dad is 55 and I am 30 this year. Your book did challenge me in my parenting, in my communicating with my family (Mom, Dad and sister). Life is precious and we don't know how many days God has given us. I miss my Dad. I'd love to cuddle up on his lap and hug his neck, like I've always done. I'd love to have a coffee with my Dad, look at him and see his loving eyes and kind face. But for now I'm happy that I can ring him or write a letter.

*Thank you for writing this book, for using your grief and loss to help others communicate before it's too late.*

> *God bless you,*
> *Grateful,*
> *Laurel B*
> *New Zealand*

## A NOTE FROM A FRIEND

MIKE: In our writing of this book, we had so many friends send us their stories and questions that they wish they could ask their own fathers if they were still alive. We found this illustration below compelling. A long-time friend and mentor of Mike, Doug Glass, lost his father, Bernard Glass at the age of 57 of lymphoma when he was 25 years young, just weeks before starting law school. He wishes he could sit down with his father one last time. He wrote us and said that if he could ask his own father 10 questions, below is what they would be for him. These are the questions Doug would want to ask:

1. Where did our family come from, why did they leave and how did they choose America?

2. How do you know if you're on the right path in life?

3. What do you consider your strongest attributes and how did they contribute to your success or failure?

4. What failures did you experience and what would you do to change it or not?

5. What values do you hold dearest and why?

6. What is the key to long term financial success?

7. What were your greatest challenges in life and how did you overcome them, if you in fact did?

8. What is it like to have people's lives literally in your hands and how did that affect your sense of self?

9. Your personal ambition seemed to predominate over your family. Why? And if you could go back and change that, would you?

10. What has given you joy in your life?

"He was the coolest guy on the planet. And he died when I was 19."

Dear Mike and Vincent,

*Questions for My Father* is something I think about often. You see, my dad died when I was 19 and it has felt like I have had to make every major life decision on my own. There has been a void in my life for 20 years. It often feels like fighting the battle of life without a wingman or without authentic support or a safety net. Imagine having to make life decisions like picking a college major, what to do after college graduation, deciding on a first job, moving to a random new city, getting engaged, getting married, buying a first house, having kids…all without the advice or opinions of the smartest guy you know. Frankly, it has been almost unbearable at times worrying about the financial challenges of life. Feeling like the financial weight of the world is on your shoulders at a young age does its damage mentally. My dad wasn't perfect but he was my idol. To me, he was the coolest guy on the planet. However, that made me a little bit intimidated by him. He was an intimidating guy. I think that caused me not to ask many questions or dig deeper into his feelings or his past. Trust me, I really could have used his advice over the years. One of the most disappointing aspects of his death was that we were just starting to connect as friends. We were just starting to have better conversations...ones that opened me up to a life I had not heard much about.

One of the things that has made me the happiest over the years is when I hear "real" stories about him. I cherish the real stories from his friends or his sister about when he was a trouble-maker, what he was like in high school, what he was like in business, what he was like around his friends. I often wonder what he would be like now as a grandfather. I wonder what our relationship would be like.

I have 3 boys of my own and I think that we have an unbelievable relationship. I do my best to draw on the memories I missed out on or on the things I wish I knew about my dad to build a strong bond with my boys. I try to tell them "real" stories about my past in high school, college, business...you know, non-dad stuff. These are the things they want to hear about the most and hang on every word and every story. They beg me for more. They remember these stories word for word. I want to make sure that my boys know the real me. I know that I used to be jealous when I would hear these stories of my dad like I missed out on something or didn't know the same guy that everyone else did. I want my boys to know me better than anyone.

Here are the questions I would ask my father if I could go back in time:

1. What was it like growing up back then? Tell me real stories about your childhood. Tell me about your friends, your parents, your aunts and uncles, your neighbors, your cars, Sunday dinners, concerts you attended, your life.

2. What was it like in high school? Let's compare notes since we sent to the same high school.

3. What was it like in Vietnam? How did you feel when you were told you had to go? What did your parents say? What were your conversations like with your parents and friends after you knew you had to go to Vietnam?

4. How did you pick your college? What jobs did you have in college? Tell me about your fraternity.

5. How did you deal with your younger brother's death? How did your family deal with it? Tell me about the day the car crash happened.

6. Tell me about your jobs after college.

7. What was your dream job?

8. Tell me about your first wife and why was it such a short relationship? Tell me about your first girlfriends.

9. Were you nervous about having a family?

10. What were your feelings when we lost our home, cars, etc. due to financial difficulty? Why did you leave? How could you let mom and me have to live in a hotel and with family members? What made you come back?

11. Tell me about your best friends in high school, college and as an adult in business.

12. What did you do day-to-day in your jobs? I try to imagine what it was like.

13. Tell me about your jobs in politics. Tell me Reagan and Sinatra stories!

14. Tell about an Italian family reunion when you were a kid.

15. Tell me about a day on the golf course with your business friends.

16. What was I like as a kid?

17. What was your proudest day as a dad?


Thanks guys! Love what you are doing.

*Mike Greco*

The Questions

## 1.

Close your eyes and picture your Dad.
What do you see first?

# 2.

Were you a confident teenager?

## 3.

---

You can go back in time in your life just
once—where do you go?

# 4.

How did you end up in your line of work?

# 5.

What do you think as you see your
children grow up?

## 6.

Has religion played any part in your life?
If yes, how?

# 7.

You see Mom for the first time—
what happens next?

# 8.

What were your parents like?

# 9.

We all die. Does that fact influence
how you live?

# 10.

Is love a fixed entity, or a work in progress?

# 11.

---

Is a total commitment to a career
a good thing?

# 12.

Is resilience something learned
or something developed?

# 13.

Patience with children—
how do you get more of it?

# 14.

Your happiest vacation—what happened?

## 15.

What would you think if I decide
not to have children?

# 16.

What's the best thing about your
favorite sport?

# 17.

What did you see on your first movie date
with Mom?

# 18.

What was it like seeing me being born?

## 19.

Tell me three things about your wedding day.

# 20.

What did your boyhood summers involve?

# 21.

Tell me about your war.

# 22.

Who's your favorite author?

# 23.

It's the morning of 9/11.
Describe the rest of your day.

# 24.

Do you miss your Dad?

# 25.

What's on your bucket list?

# 26.

Tell me how to make a decision where *everything* is on the line.

# 27.

Talk to me about the relationship between finances and life.

# 28.

Have I ever really surprised you?

# 29.

Is there really such a thing as evil?

# 30.

When someone says they're patriotic, what should that mean?

# 31.

---

Are dreams to be followed regardless of the consequences?

# 32.

Do you feel different than when you were
younger?

# 33.

When has something happened where you
were totally unprepared?

# 34.

Does society need art in order to develop?

## 35.

Can I really be anything I put my mind to?
I mean, really?

# 36.

Talk to me about growing up and
the friends you grew up with.

# 37.

Do you think you're successful?
What does that mean anyway?

# 38.

How do you know when to just quit
and do something else?

# 39.

Five seconds into the afterlife,
tell me what you're seeing.

# 40.

---

Personal integrity—tell me what that means.

# 41.

What's the point of travel?

## 42.

You're about to ask Mom to marry you. Any second thoughts?

## 43.

When was the first time you realized that the
world is a tough place to live?

## 44.

You can have dinner with three people from history—who are they? And why?

# 45.

What do you like about where you are
now in life?

# 46.

Do you miss me being a child?

# 47.

Toughest phase of parenting—
tell me what it was.

# 48.

Does forgiveness just mean forgetting?

## 49.

Which is better—being unafraid to voice my opinion or keeping my own counsel?

# 50.

Is leaving a legacy a valid aspiration?

# 51.

Should family always come before friends?

# 52.

Tell me one thing you wish you could have
changed about your Dad.

# 53.

What is courage?

# 54.

Who's your favorite comedian and why?

# 55.

It's a family gathering and you're ten years old. What do you see?

## 56.

You can have ten minutes with your Dad—
what would you say?

# 57.

---

Work/Life balance—ever get it right?
Does it exist?

# 58.

How much discipline in parenting is
too much?

# 59.

---

What do you see as my strongest trait?

## 60.

You can only listen to ten songs from now on—what are they?

# 61.

Glad you were born a guy?

# 62.

Family characteristics—
do you see any that we all share?

# 63.

Top three *Lessons Learned from being a Dad*—
tell me about them.

## 64.

What's a good example of you and Mom
working as a team to solve a problem?

## 65.

Scariest hospital visit with any of your
children—what happened?

# 66.

What did you and your friends do for fun
as teenagers?

# 67.

Would you step in and tell me if you didn't agree with my parenting?

## 68.

When was the first time you remember where
you realized you were talking to me as an
adult and not a child?

# 69.

Do you think you and Mom have shared
parenting work equally?

## 70.

You can go back and change one thing you did raising me—what is it?

## 71.

Can you imagine a version of your life where you're not a Dad?

# 72.

Who was the first girl to dump you?
How did you get over it?

## 73.

---

"My country, right or wrong"—what do you
think when you hear that?

# 74.

Tell me three things you see happening in the
world over the next twenty years.

# 75.

---

Race and racism in this country–
what's your take?

# 76.

What scares you most nowadays?

# 77.

Do you feel you know me well?

# 78.

Best Christmas ever—what happened?

## 79.

How do you figure out a way to enjoy your
children rather than worry about them?

# 80.

---

What's the trick to getting back on
the horse after a fall?

# 81.

You're driving your first car down the road.
What music is playing and where
are you going?

# 82.

---

School or Life—which one will teach
me more about who I am?

# 83.

How old were you when you started working?

## 84.

If you had the choice to become famous,
would you want to be and why?

# 85.

You've just had a perfect day.
What happened?

# 86.

Do you have a gut instinct thought as to
how you will eventually die?

# 87.

---

If you could change anything about the way
you were raised, what would it be?

# 88.

If you knew that in one year you would die,
would you change the way you are living
your life? How so and why?

# 89.

Complete this sentence: I wish I had someone
with whom I could…

# 90.

Of all the people in your family, whose death
would you find most difficult? Why?

# 91.

Social media—any tips on dealing with
THAT jungle?

## 92.

Would you recommend online dating to meet
someone in my life? Why or why not and
what's your best advice?

# 93.

What famous person do you least like
and why?

# 94.

---

Describe in detail at least five
"peak moments" in your life dating back to
your earliest memories—life events that
had a massive impact on your life journey
(for good or bad).

# 95.

Some behavior experts believe that there is one single life event that usually happens between the ages of 5 and 18 that defines who you will become as an adult. It is the biggest "peak moment" of all of them. Describe the event and how it impacted you.

# 96.

If there was one long-time friend of yours you would want me to become close with as I age, who would that be and why?

# 97.

If you were to die today, which 6 people might carry your casket? Give me one trait or lesson about each of the 6 people you would choose.

# 98.

List the friends that were in your wedding
party and tell me something about each one.

# 99.

Is there any place on the planet you haven't
been to and wish you had?

# 100.

In a given week, as a Father,
what caused you the most stress?

# 101.

If you could find out the precise date you
were to die, would you want to know or not?
Why?

## 102.

If I could hear your voice telling me
something every single morning I wake up
and every night when I go to bed,
what would you tell me?

# 103.

---

If you prayed, share your prayer and/or the specific things you prayed for.

# 104.

---

List your Top 20 words that I must teach my
children before the age of 18.

## 105.

Outside of family, who truly knows
you the best?

## 106.

What sports teams do you root for,
and how did they come to be
(college or professional sports)?

# 107.

In business or work, what were you most
known for (your "signature move")?

# 108.

In your opinion, regarding the most successful people you have met, what did they all have in common?

# 109.

You're a young boy and have just had a great day with Dad. What just happened?

# 110.

What are the Top 3 values I should live
my life by every single day?

## 111.

What one principle or rule from your
childhood do you not agree with
now as an adult?

# 112.

What is the best or funniest prank you ever
played on mom or us kids?

# 113.

If you could pick any generation to grow up
in, which one would it be and describe why?

# 114.

Briefly describe, in your view, how would you characterize each decade of life: your teens, 20's, 30's, 40's, etc.

# *Afterword*

## Vincent Staniforth:

*It's one of those rare, precious, sun-soaked English summer days. I'm walking in the hills that surround the Lancashire village where I live with my wife and young family. My Dad walks with me, and we amble along with no particular destination in mind, happy in the silence between us, conscious of the sun's warmth and the richness of the birdsong woven into the lazy air. Periodically we will stop as Dad points to a landmark in the distance, sharing a comment or an anecdote relating to his youth and travels in this same area. We don't do this often enough and I'm aware that right now, in this moment, I'm deeply contented.*

*I turn to Dad and say, "This is a good place, isn't it?" Silently surveying the gentle folds of the moorland and the views beyond, he nods and smiles. But there's a question I need to ask, and I realize it's been on my mind for a while. "We're leaving here. We're moving to the States. I think it's the right thing to do—but how do I tell if it's the best thing for us? Did you ever have to make a decision that could change everything?"*

*Before I hear an answer, the hills, birds, sunshine and wide open skies all vanish in the time it takes me to wake from the dream. I get up and start another day in Atlanta, Georgia, where we've been living for years.*

That dream, with minor variations in location and content, has recurred countless times in the years since my Dad died. It doesn't even upset me any longer; it's now simply part of my consciousness. But the same old frustration remains; I had ignored a deep, precious resource of wisdom, opinion and history because there was always another time to ask those questions, there was always going to be another phone call, another Sunday dinner, another conversation over a pint in the pub.

I'm not alone, I know, in having made that mistake. To be fair, it's a completely understandable conceit, given the brutal pace of life and the myriad demands it makes on our time, patience and resources. In fact, as a life-coping mechanism it works perfectly well—right up to the moment when it doesn't; when the phone rings in the middle of the night, when the email arrives halfway through the work day, when a relative knocks on your door unexpectedly—when it's just too damn late.

The point is simply made; the telling of stories is in our DNA. It's one of the ways we survived and developed as a species; we share our stories in order to warn, in order to educate and motivate, in order to reinforce bonds of family and friendship. But here's the thing—those stories can't be told in 140 characters or less, or in a brief social media post. We have to win back the time from life in order to be still, to think, and to tell our stories fully. We are the curators of our own histories—and it's time to pick up the pen, turn on the camera, switch on the tape recorder and tell our stories.

Tell them for posterity, tell them for our friends, tell them for our sons and daughters. *But tell them.*